Jack and the Beanstalk

from *You Read to Me, I'll Read to You*

by Mary Ann Hoberman
illustrated by Natalia Vasquez

PEARSON

Glenview, Illinois • Boston, Massachusetts • Chandler, Arizona • Upper Saddle River, New Jersey

ISBN 13: 978-0-328-47238-3
ISBN 10:   0-328-47238-7

3 4 5 6 7 8 9 10 V008 13 12 11 10

My name is Jack,
The beanstalk lad.

And I'm the ogre Jack made mad.

3

I lost our milk cow
In a trade.

You got five beans.
That's all you made.

My mother threw
Them out that night
And in the morning
What a sight!
A beanstalk grew
That was so tall
We couldn't see
The top at all.

You climbed it
To the top and then
You stole my magic
Laying hen.

Your hen that lays
Gold eggs. Why, yes.
I stole your hen,
I do confess.

My bags of gold,
You stole them, too.
And then my golden harp.

That's true.

That was a naughty Thing to do!

Now Mister Ogre,
Don't be mad.
I do admit
That I was bad,
But we were poor
And hungry, too.

12

13

I'll give them back
If you agree
To sometimes lend
Your hen to me.

14

You're asking me
To lend my hen?

Not all the time.
Just now and then.
And also for
A special treat,
Please lend your harp.
It sounds so sweet.

16

Why, yes, it has
A lovely tone.
But don't forget,
It's just a loan!

17

A bag of gold
Perhaps you'd share?

"A half-bag's all
That I can spare."

Now that's all settled
And we're friends
And that's the way
Our story ends.

Let's write it down. Let's write it now.

We'll tell about
The beans and cow

And how the beanstalk
Grew and grew

And when our story
Is all through,
You'll read to me!
I'll read to you!